MODERN MONK

Ancient Wisdom for a New Era

Zach Perlman

Library of Congress Control Number: 2018675309
Printed in the United States of America

ISBN: 9798309019519

May all beings be happy and free from suffering.

CONTENTS

PREFACE

Why This Book?

Monasticism has long stood as a pillar of spiritual discipline, a retreat from the noise of the world into the stillness of self-inquiry. The image of a monk—shaven head, simple robes, eyes gazing inward—evokes something timeless, something beyond the everyday concerns of ordinary life. Whether in a Himalayan cave, a forest monastery, or a Zen temple, monks have dedicated themselves to the pursuit of wisdom, detachment, and ultimate liberation. Their lives have symbolized the renunciation of the trivial in favor of the transcendent, a complete and deliberate turning away from the distractions that entangle the ordinary person in cycles of suffering.

But what does it mean to be a monk in the 21st century? We live in an era unlike any before it. The monastery walls have been replaced by digital landscapes, and the hermit's cave now sits among the skyscrapers of the modern world. Information flows faster than ever, our attention is constantly fragmented, and true solitude—once the foundation of spiritual practice—is a luxury few can afford. At the same time, the world is witnessing an unprecedented resurgence of interest in mindfulness, meditation, and self-transcendence. More people than ever seek clarity in a world saturated with noise, longing for depth in an existence that often feels shallow and ephemeral.

This book is not a historical account of monasticism, nor is it a manual for joining a traditional monastery. It does not aim to romanticize the past or lament the loss of an ancient way of life. Instead, it is an exploration of what monasticism can look like in a world where detachment seems impossible. It asks whether monastic principles can survive outside of traditional cloisters and whether the spirit of monasticism can be lived in a society that thrives on consumption and distraction. It is a vision of what it might mean to be a monk in this era—not by retreating from the world, but by engaging with it differently.

To understand where we are going, we must first understand where we have been. Monasticism is not a static tradition frozen in time. It has always evolved, adapting to new circumstances, responding to cultural shifts, and redefining itself as the world has changed. The monks of early Buddhist India, the Christian ascetics of the Egyptian deserts, the Hindu renunciates who wandered through forests, and the Zen practitioners who trained in mountain temples all approached renunciation differently. Each tradition carried the essence of monasticism but expressed it in ways unique to its time and place.

What, then, does modern monasticism look like? Must it still require physical renunciation, or can it be something more internal, more adaptable? Can someone maintain relationships, participate in society, and still live by monastic values? These are the questions that this book will explore. It is an invitation to step beyond the conventional, to reimagine monasticism not as an institution, but as a way of being—a deliberate and disciplined path of simplicity, wisdom, and presence.

This is a book for those who feel the monastic impulse but are unsure how to live it in today's world. It is for those who seek something deeper than material success and fleeting pleasures. It is for those who long to reclaim their attention, discipline their minds, and cultivate a state of presence that is unshaken by the chaos of modern life. If you feel drawn to this path, then perhaps you are already a modern monk. The journey ahead will not be about leaving the world behind, but about transforming your relationship with it.

Let us begin.

1: THE ESSENCE OF MONASTICISM

Monasticism has always been about one thing: renunciation. Not necessarily the rejection of the world, but the deliberate letting go of its grip. The monk walks a path of simplicity, discipline, and inner freedom, stripping away the non-essential to reveal what is truly meaningful. Across traditions, whether in Hinduism, Buddhism, Christianity, or other spiritual lineages, monastic life has centered around a commitment to transcendence—an unwavering pursuit of a reality beyond the fleeting distractions of daily existence.

Renunciation, in its deepest sense, is not about deprivation. It is not about rejecting life or imposing artificial hardship upon oneself. Rather, it is an act of clarity, an understanding that much of what people chase, accumulate, and cling to only serves to entangle them further in cycles of suffering. The monk does not renounce for the sake of renouncing, but because they see clearly that the attachments they leave behind are barriers to freedom. A monk does not strip their life of comforts because suffering is noble, but because comfort, when overindulged, dulls the sharp edge of awareness.

The path of monasticism has always been built upon discipline, a structured way of life that fosters inner clarity and deepens spiritual realization. It is not a life of mere contemplation but one of rigorous self-examination, constant refinement, and an unwavering commitment to wisdom. Meditation, prayer, study, and self-inquiry form the backbone of monastic existence, not as obligations but as necessary tools for understanding the nature of mind and reality itself.

Wisdom is the final aim—the deep, unshakable knowing that transcends conventional knowledge. It is not about accumulating information, memorizing scriptures, or engaging in intellectual debates, but about direct experience. True wisdom does not reside in words; it is lived, embodied, and deeply felt. The monk does not seek knowledge for its own sake but as a means to freedom.

Yet monasticism, in its traditional form, has always been defined by withdrawal. The monk leaves the world behind, stepping beyond the rhythms of ordinary life to dwell in spaces devoted to the sacred.

Whether in remote monasteries, mountain caves, or silent cloisters, monastic practice has long been rooted in physical separation from society. But as the world evolves, this model raises an important question: is renunciation still dependent on physical withdrawal, or can it be something more subtle, more internal?

Traditionally, monasticism has required an explicit, outward separation from the world, as though the world itself were the problem. But what if renunciation no longer requires isolation? Can one live in a city, engage with technology, work a job, and still embody the essence of a monk? Is it possible to walk the monastic path without shaving one's head, without wearing robes, without taking vows of celibacy or retreating into the silence of a monastery?

Throughout history, monasticism has adapted in unexpected ways. The Buddha himself rejected extreme asceticism, realizing that self-denial was no more liberating than indulgence. Instead, he taught the Middle Way—a balanced life of discipline without rigidity, renunciation without repression. Similarly, Hindu traditions have long recognized the role of householder yogis—practitioners who maintain families, engage in the world, and yet embody the principles of renunciation. Even Christian monastic traditions evolved over time, from the extreme asceticism of the Desert Fathers to the more engaged, service-oriented monastic orders of later centuries.

Today, we stand at a similar crossroads. The traditional model of monastic life—withdrawal from society, rigid vows, and strict isolation—may no longer be viable for many. But that does not mean monasticism itself is obsolete. On the contrary, its core principles are more relevant than ever in a world that thrives on distraction, excess, and endless stimulation.

The challenge, then, is not whether monasticism can survive in the modern world, but how it must evolve. If the past has shown us anything, it is that monasticism is not a relic of history, but a living tradition—one that continuously reshapes itself to meet the needs of those who seek something deeper.

The modern monk does not necessarily live in seclusion, nor do they have to abandon all material possessions. Instead, they cultivate an internal renunciation, a discipline of the mind rather than merely the body. They move through the world without being bound by it, engaging with modern life but refusing to be consumed by its noise. They may live in an apartment instead of a monastery, work a job instead of relying on alms, and maintain relationships instead of taking vows of celibacy, but their commitment to the monastic path is no less real.

In this book, we will explore what this new

form of monasticism might look like. We will examine how the ancient principles of renunciation, discipline, and contemplation can be lived within the complexity of modern existence. We will look at how monasticism has evolved throughout history, what it might become in the future, and, most importantly, how it can be embodied today—here and now, in the middle of life, without retreating from it.

The monastery, once defined by walls, is no longer a physical place. It is a state of mind, a way of being, a commitment to wisdom in the midst of a chaotic world. The question is no longer whether you can live as a monk in the modern era. The question is whether you are willing to.

2: THE EVOLUTION
OF MONASTICISM

Monasticism is often perceived as something ancient and unchanging, a relic from a distant past preserved in sacred traditions. It evokes images of silent monks in candlelit cloisters, renunciates meditating in Himalayan caves, and ascetics retreating to the wilderness in search of truth. Yet history tells a different story— one not of stasis but of continuous transformation. Monasticism has never been a fixed institution; it has always evolved, adapting to cultural shifts, responding to crises, and reshaping itself to meet the needs of each new era.

If the 21st century calls for a new kind of monasticism, then we must look to the past to see how monastic traditions have transformed before. The future does not emerge from nothing—it is shaped by what came before. To understand where monasticism is going, we must first examine where it has been.

The Birth of Monastic Traditions

Monasticism, in one form or another, has existed for thousands of years. Long before organized religions, ascetics and mystics sought solitude in forests, deserts, and mountains, abandoning the concerns of daily life to immerse themselves in contemplation. These early renunciates were not yet part of established monastic orders, but they embodied the same spirit—an intentional withdrawal from worldly distractions to pursue something beyond the material realm.

One of the first formalized monastic systems emerged in Buddhism. In 5th century BCE India, the Buddha rejected extreme asceticism in favor of a more balanced approach—the Middle Way—and established the *sangha*, a community of monks and nuns dedicated to a life of discipline, meditation, and wisdom. Unlike the solitary forest hermits of earlier traditions, these monastics did not live entirely in isolation; they relied on lay supporters for alms and, in turn, provided spiritual guidance to the broader community. Over time, Buddhist monasticism evolved from a wandering order to a structured institution, with monasteries becoming centers of learning, meditation, and spiritual discipline.

In Hinduism, monasticism took shape through the tradition of *sannyasa*, the path of renunciation. While some Hindu renunciates lived as solitary ascetics, others formed *mathas* (monastic institutions), preserving philosophical traditions and guiding disciples on the path of self-realization. The Advaita Vedanta tradition, established by Adi Shankaracharya in the 8th century CE, formalized monastic orders that blended rigorous intellectual study with direct spiritual practice.

Christian monasticism arose in the deserts of Egypt, where figures like St. Anthony the Great withdrew from society to live in ascetic solitude. But over time, solitary monasticism gave way to communal life, as monks and nuns formed monastic orders under structured rules. St. Benedict, in the 6th century CE, created one of the most enduring monastic systems in the West, emphasizing a life of prayer, work, and study. Benedictine monasteries became self-sufficient communities, dedicated to spiritual practice but also engaged in agriculture, education, and the preservation of knowledge.

Islamic monasticism, while distinct in form, found its expression in Sufism. Although Islam did not develop a formal monastic system like Buddhism or Christianity, Sufi orders emerged as centers of deep spiritual practice. Sufi mystics, often referred to as dervishes, emphasized direct experience of the Divine through meditation, chanting, and ascetic discipline. Some withdrew from society, while others engaged in teaching and service, demonstrating once again that monasticism does not always mean complete separation from the world.

Throughout history, monastic traditions have taken different forms, but they have all shared a common thread: the pursuit of transcendence through renunciation. Yet even as they preserved ancient wisdom, these traditions did not remain static. They adapted, expanded, and sometimes reinvented themselves in response to the needs of the times.

The Middle Ages: Monasticism at Its Peak

By the medieval period, monasticism had become a powerful force in both Eastern and Western traditions. In the Buddhist world, monasteries flourished as vast centers of learning, housing scholars, philosophers, and meditators who preserved sacred texts and developed new philosophical systems. Tibetan Buddhism, in particular, evolved a complex monastic structure that blended deep meditation with rigorous study and debate.

In the Christian West, monasticism played a crucial role in preserving knowledge during the so-called Dark Ages. Monastic scribes copied ancient manuscripts, keeping alive the wisdom of Greek, Roman, and early Christian thinkers. Orders such as the Franciscans and Dominicans took monastic ideals beyond the cloister, living among the people and engaging in teaching, charity, and social reform.

Sufi monasticism also flourished during this period, with mystics forming brotherhoods that combined inner contemplation with poetic expression and public teaching. Figures like Rumi, Al-Ghazali, and Ibn Arabi redefined Islamic spirituality, blending monastic discipline with profound philosophical insight.

The lesson here is clear: monasticism has never been a single, rigid model. It has evolved in response to cultural, intellectual, and spiritual needs. Monasteries have sometimes been places of withdrawal, but they have also been centers of engagement, shaping societies while remaining devoted to the pursuit of higher truth.

The Modern Challenge: Secularization and Technology

As the modern era dawned, traditional monasticism faced a crisis. The rise of secularism, scientific rationalism, and industrialization eroded the central role that religious institutions once played in society. Monasteries declined in influence, and fewer people felt drawn to the strict vows and secluded life of monastic renunciation.

At the same time, globalization and urbanization transformed the landscape of spiritual practice. Where once monastics sought refuge in remote forests and deserts, now the world itself had become interconnected, fast-paced, and relentlessly stimulating. The challenge of renunciation was no longer just about leaving society—it was about navigating a world where distraction was omnipresent.

Yet monasticism did not vanish. Instead, it began to evolve in new ways. In the 20th and 21st centuries, new movements arose that hinted at the next phase of monasticism. Thich Nhat Hanh's concept of Engaged Buddhism offered a vision of monasticism integrated with social activism, showing that renunciation need not mean retreat. The Neo-Vedanta movement, led by figures like Swami Vivekananda, redefined Hindu monasticism as a path not only of meditation but also of service to humanity. Digital monasticism began to emerge, as spiritual teachers and monks used technology to share wisdom, leading online retreats and creating virtual communities of seekers.

Toward a Modern Monasticism

Every era has redefined monasticism to meet the needs of its time. The 21st century is no different. As traditional monasteries decline, new possibilities emerge. Some monks are choosing to live in cities, integrating renunciation with modern life. Lay monastic movements are forming, where individuals take on monastic-style disciplines while remaining engaged with family, career, and society.

Digital monasteries are appearing, using technology to build global communities dedicated to deep spiritual practice.

The monastic ideal has never been about the place —it has always been about the mindset. If the old monastery walls are dissolving, then the challenge of our time is to cultivate renunciation, discipline, and wisdom in new ways. The question is not whether monasticism will survive, but how it will transform.

The next chapter will explore this transformation in greater detail, examining the emerging possibilities for a new kind of monkhood—one that embraces the timeless essence of monastic practice while adapting to the realities of the modern world.

3: MONASTIC PRACTICES ACROSS CULTURES

Monasticism is not confined to any one tradition. Across the world, different cultures have cultivated their own expressions of renunciation, asceticism, and contemplative life. While the outward forms vary, the core essence remains the same—a deep commitment to spiritual realization through discipline, simplicity, and detachment from the distractions of the world.

In some traditions, monasticism takes the form of strict communal life, with clearly defined rules and rituals that guide every moment of the day. In others, it manifests as radical solitude, with renunciates wandering alone, free from institutional ties. Some monastic paths emphasize rigorous intellectual study, while others cultivate direct mystical experience. Some renunciates seek purity in silence, fasting, and prayer; others embrace engagement with the world, treating every experience as part of their spiritual training.

By exploring the diversity of monastic traditions, we can see that monasticism is not a single rigid formula but a living practice that adapts to its cultural and historical context. More importantly, modern seekers can draw from these traditions, incorporating their wisdom into contemporary life in ways that resonate with our unique time and place.

The Buddhist Monk: The Disciplined Wanderer and the Meditative Scholar

Buddhist monasticism is among the oldest and most structured forms of renunciation, originating with the establishment of the *sangha* by the Buddha. But even within Buddhism, the practice of monasticism takes on vastly different forms.

In the Theravāda tradition, prevalent in Southeast Asia, monks embrace a life of extreme simplicity. They own almost nothing—just a robe, a begging bowl, and a few personal essentials. Relying on daily alms from laypeople, they cultivate a radical interdependence between the monastic and the household worlds. Their days are spent in meditation, scriptural study, and mindful presence, following the *Vinaya*, a set of monastic precepts that govern their behavior with meticulous detail.

In Zen Buddhism, monastic life is centered around rigorous meditation training, often in highly structured monasteries. Zen monks endure long hours of seated meditation (*zazen*), sometimes spending years in silent retreat before reaching deeper levels of realization. Yet Zen practice is not limited to the meditation hall. Every action—chopping wood, carrying water, cooking, sweeping—becomes an expression of mindfulness. The monastery itself functions as a kind of living meditation, where the most ordinary tasks are performed with absolute presence.

Tibetan Buddhist monasticism blends deep philosophical study with esoteric tantric practices. Monks engage in years of intensive debate, mastering intricate philosophical arguments, while also training in visualization, mantra recitation, and yogic exercises like *tummo*, the practice of generating inner heat. Some enter three-year, three-month, and three-day solitary retreats, emerging with a transformed consciousness that few outside the tradition can comprehend.

Each of these Buddhist monastic paths teaches a unique lesson. The begging monk of Theravāda Buddhism shows that renunciation is not about personal deprivation but about freeing oneself from the illusion of ownership. The Zen monk demonstrates that enlightenment is found not in theory but in direct, embodied experience. The Tibetan scholar-monk reminds us that wisdom must be rigorously cultivated through both study and deep inner practice.

The Hindu Sannyasi: The Wandering Renunciate

In Hinduism, monasticism takes many forms, but at its heart is the tradition of *sannyasa*, the path of total renunciation. Unlike Buddhist monks, who live within monastic institutions, many Hindu renunciates abandon all ties to monasteries, families, and possessions, living as wandering ascetics.

The *Advaita Vedanta* sannyasi sees the world as an illusion (*maya*), dedicating themselves to dissolving the false sense of individual identity. Their practice centers on self-inquiry (*atma vichara*), asking the fundamental question: "Who am I?" Through this relentless questioning, they seek to transcend the illusion of separateness and merge with the absolute (*Brahman*).

At the other extreme are the *Aghoris*, the radical renunciates of Tantra, who meditate in cremation grounds to transcend fear and attachment. Rather than rejecting the body, emotions, or so-called impurity, they embrace everything as sacred. Their practice is a direct confrontation with the conditioned mind, challenging every boundary and taboo.

Both paths, despite their differences, reveal a fundamental truth about renunciation. One teaches that detachment from illusion leads to ultimate freedom. The other teaches that nothing is truly separate, and liberation comes not from rejection but from total acceptance.

The Christian Monk: The Devotional Seeker

Christian monasticism, particularly in the Benedictine tradition, is based on the principles of prayer, work, and study. Unlike the solitary ascetics of the early Christian deserts, who lived in caves and practiced extreme self-denial, Benedictine monks created structured communities where discipline and devotion could flourish.

The monastic day is divided into strict periods of prayer, manual labor, and study. The Rule of St. Benedict emphasizes humility, silence, and obedience, recognizing that true spiritual depth requires not only prayer but also action. The monastery itself functions as a self-sustaining world, a place where every action—whether farming, cooking, or copying manuscripts—becomes a sacred offering.

In contrast, the Eastern Orthodox tradition developed a more mystical approach through the practice of *hesychasm*. Monks in Greece, Russia, and Egypt withdrew into deep silence, repeating the

Jesus Prayer ("Lord Jesus Christ, have mercy on me") as a method of inner purification. Their goal was not just intellectual knowledge but direct experience of the Divine—a process that required years, if not a lifetime, of dedicated practice.

Christian monasticism teaches that renunciation is not just about withdrawing from the world but about transforming it. It demonstrates that devotion, discipline, and humility can create an inner monastery, regardless of where one lives.

The Taoist Hermit: The Natural Mystic

Taoist monasticism in China evolved as a path of effortless harmony with the *Dao*—the fundamental principle of existence. Unlike the strict discipline of Buddhist or Christian monasticism, Taoist monks often lived alone in the mountains, practicing meditation, energy cultivation, and martial arts.

Rather than rigid asceticism, Taoist practice emphasizes spontaneity and balance. The goal is not to force enlightenment through effort but to align oneself with the natural flow of life. Meditation is not about controlling the mind but about observing it. Physical practices like *qigong* cultivate internal energy, allowing the body and spirit to move in harmony.

This tradition reminds us that renunciation need not be rigid or austere. Sometimes, the highest wisdom is found not in struggle, but in surrender.

A Universal Monastic Wisdom

Despite their differences, all monastic traditions share a core wisdom:

Monks renounce not to escape the world, but to see it clearly.

They embrace discipline not as self-punishment, but as a path to inner freedom.

They cultivate silence, solitude, and contemplation, knowing that truth is found in stillness.

Each tradition offers a unique perspective, yet they all point to the same essential reality—that lasting peace and wisdom arise when one lets go of the unnecessary and embraces the present moment fully.

The modern monk does not need to choose a single tradition. Instead, they can draw from all of them, integrating what resonates and adapting monastic wisdom to the realities of contemporary life. The monastery may no longer be a walled institution, but its essence—simplicity, clarity, and depth—can be lived anywhere.

As we move forward, we will explore what it means to bring these monastic values into the modern world. The question is no longer whether monasticism can survive outside its historical traditions, but how it must evolve to meet the needs of those walking the path today.

4: THE ROLE OF COMMUNITY IN MODERN MONASTICISM

Monasticism has traditionally been a path of solitude, yet even the most dedicated renunciates have never walked it entirely alone. From the Buddhist sangha to the Christian monastic orders, communal life has played a vital role in shaping, supporting, and preserving the monastic path. The archetype of the lone hermit, meditating in a cave or wandering through forests, is only part of the monastic story. In reality, monasticism has always existed in a delicate balance between solitude and community, withdrawal and connection.

But what happens when monasteries no longer define the landscape of monastic life? How does the modern monk find fellowship, accountability, and support without traditional monastic structures?

In a world where renunciation no longer means retreating to a mountaintop, how do seekers cultivate a sense of belonging while walking an unconventional path?

This chapter explores the tension between solitude and connection, the necessity of spiritual friendship, and the ways modern monasticism can adapt without losing the power of communal wisdom.

The Tension Between Solitude and Connection

Throughout history, monastic traditions have wrestled with a fundamental question: *Is enlightenment best pursued alone, or within a community?* The answer, as with most things, is not absolute. Some traditions emphasize radical solitude, while others recognize the deep value of spiritual companionship. Both approaches have their strengths and pitfalls.

The solitary path has always been held in high regard. The Desert Fathers and Mothers of early Christianity withdrew to the Egyptian wilderness to escape the corruption of society. They believed that the distractions of communal life—conversation, social obligations, even friendships—interfered with the purity of their spiritual focus. Similarly, Zen monks have long valued deep periods of solitary retreat, where direct realization arises only when all external influences are stripped away. Hindu sannyasis and Aghoris also embrace extreme detachment, rejecting not only material possessions but all social norms and ties.

Yet solitude, taken to an extreme, can become a form of escapism. The human mind, left unchallenged, has a tendency to create its own illusions. Even the most disciplined practitioners are not immune to self-deception, spiritual stagnation, or the slow erosion of motivation. Without others to reflect their blind spots, even the most sincere renunciates can fall into patterns of arrogance, complacency, or delusion.

On the other hand, communal monasticism provides structure, accountability, and a shared sense of purpose. The Buddhist *sangha* serves as a network of support, ensuring that no monk walks the path alone. Christian monastic orders function like families, where each member plays a role in maintaining the stability of the whole. Sufi brotherhoods emphasize group chanting, storytelling, and devotional practice, fostering a sense of unity that strengthens individual spiritual progress.

But communal life has its challenges as well. Rules can become rigid, stifling genuine insight. Group dynamics can introduce power struggles, distractions, and conflicts. The weight of an institution can sometimes overshadow the original spiritual impulse that brought seekers together in the first place. Community, while invaluable, is not always free of pitfalls.

For the modern seeker, the challenge is finding the right balance—integrating both solitude and connection into the monastic journey.

The Need for Spiritual Friendship

The Buddha once told his disciple Ananda, *"Spiritual friendship is not half of the holy life, Ananda. It is the whole of the holy life."* This statement underscores a profound truth: even the most dedicated practitioner benefits from the companionship of like-minded seekers.

Spiritual friendship is not the same as ordinary social connection. It is not based on shared hobbies, entertainment, or personal interests. It is rooted in a mutual commitment to wisdom, discipline, and awakening. A true spiritual friend is one who encourages deeper practice, holds space for honest reflection, and helps navigate the challenges of the path.

In the modern world, where traditional monastic communities are rare, spiritual friendships become even more essential. They provide the support and accountability that monasteries once offered, without requiring complete withdrawal from the world. Whether found in local meditation groups, online forums, or one-on-one mentorships, these relationships form the backbone of a modern monastic network.

The challenge, of course, is finding such friendships in a society that prioritizes superficial connection over depth. In a world where most relationships revolve around entertainment, productivity, or distraction, true spiritual companionship is rare. Yet it is precisely this rarity that makes it so valuable.

For those seeking spiritual friendship, the first step is to create space for it. Attending meditation retreats, participating in philosophical discussions, or simply being open about one's monastic aspirations can attract others on a similar path. If no community exists, building one—even if it begins with just two or three committed individuals—can be a powerful step toward creating a modern monastic network.

Digital Sanghas and Online Monastic Communities

Technology has changed everything—including monastic life. In the past, monks lived together in monasteries, bound by physical proximity. Today, seekers are finding community in digital spaces, connecting across continents, sharing wisdom, and supporting one another without ever meeting in person.

The rise of digital monasticism is an unexpected but natural evolution. Online meditation groups provide daily practice sessions, allowing individuals to maintain consistency even when physically isolated. Virtual retreats offer deep study and discipline without the need for travel. Social media, often criticized for its distractions, has also become a tool for spreading monastic teachings, building global sanghas, and fostering discussions that might not have been possible a generation ago.

Yet digital community comes with its own set of challenges. The very technology that connects can also fragment attention. Without the physical presence of others, accountability may weaken, and the depth of connection can sometimes feel hollow. Unlike a traditional monastery, where shared discipline creates an immersive environment, online spaces require greater self-discipline to remain truly engaged.

Despite these limitations, the digital monastery is a growing reality. Many seekers now take vows, live disciplined lives, and support one another entirely through online communities. For some, this is a temporary bridge until they find a physical sangha. For others, it represents the future of monastic life —a decentralized, global network of practitioners walking the path together.

The Power of the Modern Ashram

While traditional monasteries are in decline, a new model is emerging: the urban ashram. Unlike the isolated monasteries of the past, these spaces exist within cities, open to both renunciates and lay practitioners. They function as sanctuaries of wisdom and discipline, providing structured practice without requiring permanent vows.

Modern ashrams often blend monastic principles with contemporary flexibility. They allow seekers to immerse themselves in spiritual training for weeks, months, or even years, without the expectation of lifelong commitment. Some function as co-living spaces, where residents dedicate themselves to meditation, study, and service. Others operate as retreat centers, offering temporary monastic experiences for those who wish to step away from daily life for periods of deep practice.

This hybrid model—part monastery, part retreat center, part intentional community—may well represent the future of monasticism. It provides the structure and support of a traditional monastic environment while remaining accessible to those who cannot fully renounce the world.

Conclusion: Walking Together, Even in Solitude

A modern monk may practice alone, but they are never truly alone. The sangha has evolved—it now exists across time and space. The monastery has changed—it is now the home, the retreat, the online gathering. The path of solitude is real—but so is the need for connection.

Monasticism has always required both aloneness and togetherness. The modern monk must learn to navigate this balance—embracing solitude when needed, and seeking wisdom in community when the time is right.

The future of monasticism may not be in grand monasteries or remote retreats. It may be in the quiet friendships between seekers, in the digital spaces where wisdom is shared, in the small communities where renunciates and householders walk the path side by side. What remains unchanged is the core truth: enlightenment is not an individual pursuit. It is a path we walk together.

As we move forward, we will explore how monastic principles can be fully integrated into modern life. The question is no longer whether monasticism can adapt—it is how each of us will embody it.

5: A NEW MONASTIC VISION

Monasticism is not dead. It is simply waiting to be reborn.

For centuries, monasteries stood as bastions of spiritual discipline, shielding seekers from the distractions of the world so they could pursue awakening with unwavering focus. The traditional monastic model, with its vows, seclusion, and strict routines, offered a clear and structured path. But the world has changed. Today's seekers live in a vastly different reality, one where renunciation no longer means withdrawing into the wilderness but learning to navigate the complexities of modern life with clarity, discipline, and presence.

If the traditional monastery no longer serves as the primary structure for monastic life, what could take its place? What does it mean to be a monk in an era of constant connectivity, economic pressures, and technological acceleration? How can monastic wisdom be preserved while embracing the realities of the 21st century?

This chapter explores a vision for modern monasticism—a way of living that upholds the timeless principles of renunciation, contemplation, and discipline while adapting them to a world that looks nothing like the past.

What Does It Mean to Be a Monk Today?

If a monk is not defined by robes, a monastery, or institutional vows, then what remains? The essence of monasticism has never been in its outward trappings but in the quality of one's inner life. A monk is not simply someone who withdraws from the world but one who renounces illusion, distraction, and attachment in pursuit of something deeper.

To be a modern monk is to live with intention in an age of chaos. It is to cultivate simplicity while surrounded by complexity, to practice stillness in a world addicted to movement. It is to reject the noise of consumerism, status-seeking, and compulsive distraction—not by escaping from society, but by transforming one's relationship to it.

The new monasticism does not ask, *What must I give up?* but rather, *What truly matters?* It does not seek refuge in ritual for its own sake but in the disciplined refinement of awareness. It is a path not of rejection but of conscious engagement, where every action is infused with clarity and purpose.

The Four Pillars of a Modern Monastic Life

A new kind of monkhood must adapt while remaining rooted in the timeless foundations of monasticism. The following four pillars outline a possible framework:

1. Renunciation: Letting Go Without Withdrawing

Traditional monasticism demanded radical external renunciation—giving up family, wealth, possessions, and personal identity. The modern monk, however, practices a more internal form of renunciation, one that does not require abandoning the world but rather loosening its grip.

This renunciation is not about deprivation but discernment. It is about recognizing what truly serves the path and what entangles the mind in cycles of craving and suffering. A modern monk may own a smartphone but renounces compulsive scrolling. They may engage in relationships but release attachment to validation and control. They may live in a city but cultivate an inner solitude untouched by its distractions.

Renunciation is not about what is left behind, but about what is gained—freedom, clarity, and an unshakable peace that is not dependent on external conditions.

2. Contemplation: A Life of Inner Work

Monastic life has always centered on deep contemplation, whether through meditation, prayer, or self-inquiry. The modern monk carries this tradition forward, making space for stillness and inner exploration in a world that constantly demands outward attention.

This may take the form of daily meditation, silent retreats, or simple moments of intentional presence woven into everyday life. It is not about withdrawing into thought but about cutting through illusion, piercing the layers of conditioning that obscure reality.

Contemplation, in its truest sense, is not passive. It is the active cultivation of wisdom, the practice of seeing clearly and living accordingly.

3. Discipline: Structure in a Chaotic World

Traditional monks lived by strict schedules, bound by vows that dictated every aspect of their lives. While the modern monk may not live under monastery rules, discipline remains essential. Without structure, the mind drifts into distraction, and the path becomes vague and uncertain.

Discipline is not about restriction but liberation. By setting clear boundaries—daily meditation, mindful eating, intentional solitude—the modern monk creates a framework that supports clarity and deepens awareness. This discipline is not externally imposed but internally chosen, a commitment to cultivating freedom rather than being enslaved by impulse.

A modern monk does not need to follow ancient rituals, but they do need rhythm, consistency, and commitment to practice.

4. Service: Engagement Without Attachment

While traditional monasticism often emphasized retreat, the modern monk is called to engage. The world is in crisis—not just materially, but spiritually. There is a hunger for meaning, a deep longing for something beyond the shallow distractions of contemporary life. Monastic wisdom has never been more relevant.

The modern monk recognizes that awakening is not just personal but collective. They bring the monastery into the world, sharing insight, teaching, creating, and offering service in whatever form aligns with their gifts. Whether through writing, mentorship, activism, or simple acts of kindness, their presence itself becomes an offering.

But engagement without attachment is key. The modern monk does not serve out of obligation or ego but as a natural expression of wisdom. They give without seeking reward, act without clinging to results, and share their knowledge freely without needing recognition.

Service is not separate from the monastic path—it is its completion.

Forms of Modern Monasticism

How might this vision manifest in reality? Here are three possible models for a new kind of monkhood:

1. The Urban Monk: Living Monastically in Society

Some modern monks will choose to live simply within the world, integrating monastic values into daily life. They might live in small, minimalist spaces, wake before dawn to meditate, and structure their days around deep study and contemplation. Their work—whether as teachers, writers, or creatives—is an extension of their practice, approached with full presence and detachment from egoic ambition.

2. The Lay Monastic Order: A New Kind of Sangha

Others may seek community, forming small groups of dedicated practitioners who live by shared principles. These modern monastic networks could function as lay monastic orders, where members take vows of simplicity, meditation, and ethical living while remaining integrated within society. Unlike traditional monastic orders, these communities could be decentralized, flexible, and open to both renunciates and householders.

3. The Digital Monk: Spreading Wisdom Without Walls

Technology has created a new possibility—the global, digital monastery. Some modern monks will take their practice online, using digital platforms to build sanghas, lead virtual retreats, and share teachings with seekers worldwide. This path allows wisdom to reach those who might never step foot in a physical monastery, bringing monastic insight into the heart of modern life.

Each of these models preserves the essence of monasticism while adapting to contemporary realities. None is superior; what matters is the sincerity of practice and the depth of commitment.

Conclusion: A Call to the New Monastics

This book is not just a reflection on monasticism's past—it is an invitation to help shape its future.

If you feel the monastic impulse within you—if you long for a life of contemplation, simplicity, and wisdom—then you are already on this path. The question is not whether you can be a monk in the modern world, but how you will embody it.

The new monasticism will not be built in stone temples or walled monasteries. It will emerge wherever there are seekers willing to live with intention, discipline, and presence. It will take shape in urban apartments, rural retreats, digital spaces, and small circles of committed practitioners. It will not be defined by external appearances but by the clarity of mind and depth of insight cultivated by those who walk this path.

The future of monasticism is not in the past. It is in those who choose to live it now.

Are you ready to take the first step?

6: LIVING THE MONASTIC LIFE WITHOUT A MONASTERY

Monastic life has long been associated with retreat—hidden temples, isolated hermitages, and silent cloisters far removed from the distractions of the world. The image of the monk is often one of radical separation, a figure who turns away from society to seek something higher. Yet for many modern seekers, this kind of withdrawal is neither practical nor desirable. Responsibilities, relationships, and financial realities make traditional monastic renunciation unattainable for most.

But what if renunciation was never about leaving the world? What if the essence of monastic life could be embodied within ordinary existence? What if the monastery was not a physical place, but a way of being?

For the modern monk, the challenge is not escaping to the mountains but learning to cultivate monastic discipline in the midst of daily life. The question is not how to live in a monastery, but how to transform one's life into a monastery—one defined not by walls, vows, or rituals, but by clarity, simplicity, and deep presence.

Creating a Personal Monastery

If a monastery is a space for deep spiritual work, then the modern monk must learn to cultivate that space wherever they are. This requires both external and internal shifts—structuring one's environment and mind in ways that support the contemplative path.

The Outer Monastery: Structuring Your Physical Space

Traditional monasteries are designed to minimize distraction and maximize clarity. They are intentionally simple, free of unnecessary possessions, and arranged to support meditation, study, and contemplation. The modern monk, though living outside a monastery, can create a similar environment.

The first step is reducing external clutter. A clear, ordered space mirrors a clear, ordered mind. This does not mean living with nothing, but rather keeping only what is useful, meaningful, or deeply valued. A minimalist approach—not for aesthetic reasons, but for functional ones—helps remove the unconscious weight of excess.

Beyond simplicity, the modern monk benefits from having a dedicated space for practice. This need not be an entire room—it can be a single corner, a cushion, an altar, or a desk used only for meditation and contemplation. The key is consistency. Just as monastics have designated places for prayer and study, the modern monk benefits from creating an environment that signals to the mind: *This is a space for depth.*

Symbols of renunciation—whether books, sacred objects, or intentional design choices—can also serve as reminders of the path. The goal is not to replicate a monastery but to shape one's surroundings in a way that reinforces inner discipline.

The Inner Monastery: Cultivating Mental Space

Physical simplicity is only the first step. The true monastery is internal, built not of stone but of mindfulness. Without external structures enforcing discipline, the modern monk must cultivate internal boundaries.

Mental simplicity means training the mind to detach from unnecessary thoughts, anxieties, and distractions. In a world designed to fragment attention, this is no small task. It requires deliberate effort to minimize exposure to noise—both literal and informational. This may mean reducing media consumption, limiting social interactions that do not serve one's path, or practicing intentional solitude even in a busy life.

Just as monasteries have set times for prayer, the modern monk benefits from structured moments of stillness. Whether it is a daily meditation practice, a silent morning routine, or designated periods of solitude, these practices help create mental space within the chaos of everyday existence.

Renunciation, in this context, does not mean withdrawing from life but choosing how to engage with it. It is the ability to move through the world without being consumed by it, to experience life fully while remaining inwardly free.

Renunciation in the Modern World

Traditional monks renounce material wealth, family life, and worldly ambitions. But the modern monk practices a different kind of renunciation—one suited to life in a connected, fast-paced world.

What to Renounce: Not Objects, But Attachments

Renunciation in the modern era is less about giving up physical possessions and more about relinquishing attachment to them. It is about letting go of the compulsive need for validation, the addiction to busyness, and the relentless pursuit of external achievements.

This form of renunciation involves stepping away from compulsive entertainment, news cycles, and digital distractions. It means questioning habits that drain energy and attention, from excessive consumption to habitual socializing. It is not about rejecting enjoyment but about recognizing when pleasure becomes dependency.

True renunciation is not deprivation—it is freedom. It is the realization that nothing external can provide lasting fulfillment and the choice to invest energy in what truly matters.

What to Cultivate Instead: The Monastic Alternative

When renouncing attachment, what remains? In place of distraction, the modern monk cultivates presence. In place of excessive consumption, they embrace simplicity. In place of self-centered ambition, they practice service and wisdom.

This does not mean rejecting all comforts or conveniences, but rather using them consciously. A modern monk may use technology, but they are not enslaved by it. They may have relationships, but they do not base their identity on them. They may work, create, and engage with the world, but they do so with clarity and non-attachment.

Monasticism is not about rejecting life—it is about reclaiming it from illusion.

A Modern Monastic Discipline

Traditional monasteries impose structure, schedules, and vows. Without these external forms, the modern monk must create their own discipline —a self-imposed framework that supports deep practice.

Daily Monastic Practices

To embody monastic values, the modern monk benefits from daily rituals that anchor the path. This might include:

Morning meditation to establish clarity before engaging with the world.

Silent reflection at set points in the day, providing moments of stillness amid activity.

Sacred study of wisdom texts, philosophy, or contemplative literature.

Mindful work—whether writing, teaching, or physical labor—performed with full presence.

Service and compassion as an expression of wisdom, not obligation.

Evening closure, reviewing the day with gratitude and releasing unnecessary thoughts.

These practices do not need to be rigid or time-consuming. What matters is consistency—a commitment to structuring life around depth rather than distraction.

Self-Imposed Vows: Flexible Yet Firm Commitments

Without formal vows, the modern monk can create their own commitments, choosing disciplines that align with their path. These may include:

- A vow of **mindful consumption**, choosing only what nourishes the mind and spirit.
- A vow of **silence**, maintaining periods of quiet to cultivate inner awareness.
- A vow of **presence**, engaging fully in each task, conversation, and action.
- A vow of **simplicity**, reducing excess in both possessions and commitments.The purpose of these vows is not restriction but liberation. They serve as guiding principles, helping to refine awareness and minimize distraction.

Integrating Monasticism Into Work and Relationships

Monastic life is often seen as a rejection of work, relationships, and engagement with the world. But the modern monk does not withdraw—they transform these aspects into part of the spiritual path.

Monasticism in Work: Turning Labor Into Practice

Work, when approached with mindfulness, can be a form of meditation. Whether sweeping floors in a monastery or answering emails in an office, the principle remains the same—performing each task with full awareness, free from grasping at results.

Monasticism in Relationships: Engaging Without Attachment

The modern monk does not reject relationships but approaches them with non-attachment. They love deeply, but without possessiveness. They communicate with intention, avoiding unnecessary speech. They balance solitude and connection, understanding when to engage and when to withdraw into silence.

Conclusion: Walking the Path Without Leaving the World

The monastery is not a place—it is a way of being.

A modern monk does not need to retreat to the mountains or shave their head. Instead, they carry the monastery within them, turning everyday life into a sacred space.

The path is not about rejecting the world, but about moving through it with wisdom, clarity, and peace. The next chapter will explore where monasticism is headed—how technology, globalization, and societal changes may shape the next evolution of the monastic path.

7: THE HUMAN BODY AND THE MONASTIC PATH

For centuries, monasticism has been associated with transcendence—the idea that spiritual practice is about rising above the body, leaving behind its desires, and focusing solely on the mind or soul. Many traditions have viewed the body as a temporary vessel, something to be subdued, ignored, or even punished in pursuit of enlightenment. In extreme ascetic traditions, monks have fasted for weeks, sat motionless for days, or endured physical austerities to sever attachment to the physical self.

But is this really the highest approach?

The modern monk lives in a world where science, health, and holistic well-being are better understood than ever before. If monasticism is to evolve, it must also reconsider the body's role in the spiritual path. Instead of treating the body as an obstacle to enlightenment, it can be seen as a vital part of the journey—a tool for deepening awareness, strengthening discipline, and refining perception.

This chapter explores how physical discipline, health, and embodiment can become integral parts of modern monastic life.

The Traditional View of the Body in Monasticism

Throughout history, monastic traditions have had widely varying relationships with the body. Some have embraced extreme asceticism, while others have incorporated movement, physical training, or energy cultivation as part of their path. By examining these different approaches, we can understand how they apply to modern monasticism.

The Ascetic Approach: Rejecting the Body

Some monastic traditions have viewed the body as an obstacle to spiritual realization, something to be transcended or renounced entirely.

In Hinduism, sadhus and renunciates often engage in extreme austerities (*tapas*), such as prolonged fasting, holding a single arm in the air for years, or living in complete isolation. The idea is that by mastering physical suffering, the practitioner weakens attachment to the body and dissolves identification with the physical self.

In early Christianity, the Desert Fathers and Mothers practiced self-mortification, sleeping on hard ground, wearing chains, and even inflicting physical pain to discipline the body's desires.

In Buddhism, particularly in its earliest forms, monks were encouraged to eat only once a day, wear robes made of discarded cloth, and endure hardship without complaint. Some monastics practiced *dhutanga*, extreme renunciations like living outdoors year-round or refusing to lie down when sleeping.

These practices, while demonstrating remarkable discipline, often led to suffering rather than liberation. Even the Buddha himself abandoned extreme asceticism after realizing that starving the body only weakens the mind. His insight—that enlightenment comes not through indulgence or denial but through balance—laid the foundation for the Middle Way.

Lesson for the Modern Monk: The ability to endure discomfort is valuable, but extreme physical denial can be counterproductive. A disciplined yet balanced approach to the body serves the path far better than rigid austerities.

The Balanced Approach: Honoring the Body

Other traditions have recognized that the body is not something to be rejected but something to be understood and integrated into spiritual practice.

In Taoism, the body is seen as an extension of the natural world, and maintaining its balance is essential for cultivating harmony with the Dao. Practices like *qigong* and *tai chi* focus on moving energy (*qi*) through the body, refining awareness and strengthening the connection between body and mind.

In Tibetan Buddhism, physical exercises like *tummo* (inner heat meditation) harness the body's energy to deepen meditative absorption. Advanced practitioners can regulate their body temperature, enabling them to meditate for hours in freezing conditions without discomfort.

In Hindu Yoga, the body is not an obstacle but a vehicle for awakening. Yogis use breath control (*pranayama*), postures (*asanas*), and inner locks (*bandhas*) to refine physical and mental awareness, preparing for deep meditation.

Each of these traditions treats the body not as a hindrance but as an essential part of the spiritual journey.

Lesson for the Modern Monk: The body, when trained and disciplined, can be a powerful ally in spiritual practice. It does not need to be transcended; it needs to be understood.

The Role of Physical Health in Monasticism

A weak or sick body can be a major obstacle to practice. While renouncing worldly comforts is part of the monastic path, neglecting health is not. Strength, resilience, and vitality support deeper meditation, focus, and discipline.

Food as a Spiritual Practice

Traditional monastic diets are often simple, intentional, and guided by principles of mindfulness and moderation.

- Buddhist monks in the Theravāda tradition follow an *alms-round diet*, eating only what is offered to them, reinforcing detachment from food cravings.
- Christian monastic orders have practiced fasting and mindful eating, treating meals as sacred rather than indulgent.
- Hindu sannyasis often follow vegetarian or sattvic diets, avoiding foods that are overly stimulating or dulling to the mind.

For the modern monk, food can be approached with the same awareness. It is not about rigid dietary rules but about conscious consumption—eating not for pleasure alone but to sustain the body for practice.

Monastic Approach to Eating in Modern Life:

- Choose simple, nutritious foods that sustain without overstimulation.
- Eat mindfully, with gratitude and full awareness.
- Avoid excess, recognizing when food is being used for comfort rather than nourishment.

Physical Training as a Monastic Discipline

While monks are often pictured sitting in meditation, many traditions incorporate physical training as part of their path.

- Shaolin monks train rigorously in martial arts, viewing movement as a form of meditation.
- Taoist monks practice qigong to refine their energy and increase longevity.
- Yogis use postures to develop discipline, endurance, and bodily control.

The modern monk can adopt a similar philosophy —engaging in physical training not for vanity or competition but as a practice of discipline and awareness.

Modern Monastic Training Approaches:

- Yoga or Qigong: Cultivating flexibility, balance, and inner energy.
- Strength Training or Calisthenics: Building resilience and endurance.
- Walking Meditation or Hiking: Using movement as a tool for contemplation.

Movement, when approached with awareness, is not separate from meditation—it is meditation in motion.

Sleep and Recovery: The Forgotten Discipline

Monks are often portrayed as waking before dawn, sleeping little, and dedicating all their time to practice. While discipline is important, sleep deprivation does not lead to enlightenment. The Dalai Lama has said that sleep, when done consciously, is itself a form of meditation.

A modern monk's approach to rest should be just as disciplined as their approach to work or meditation.

Monastic Approach to Sleep:

- Maintain a consistent wake-up time, reinforcing structure.
- Treat sleep as sacred, avoiding distractions before bed.
- Create a simple, quiet environment for rest, free from technology.

Rather than seeing sleep as wasted time, the modern monk views it as essential renewal.

Avoiding the Extremes: Neither Indulgence Nor Repression

21st-century culture often swings between two extremes—overindulgence and self-punishment. Modern consumerism glorifies excess, while some spiritual traditions promote unnecessary suffering. Neither approach leads to wisdom.

The **Middle Path for the Modern Monk** is simple:

- Eat, but don't overeat.
- Train, but don't obsess.
- Rest, but don't become lazy.

Spirituality is not about rejecting the body—it is about mastering it.

Conclusion: The Body as a Sacred Temple

The body is not separate from the spiritual path—it is the path. It is the monastery in which consciousness dwells. Neglecting the body weakens the mind. Obsessing over the body distracts from wisdom. But caring for the body with awareness strengthens both.

The modern monk does not reject the body. They discipline it, respect it, and use it as a tool for awakening. The monastery is not a distant retreat—it is here, in this very body, in this very breath.

Treat the body as a sacred monastery. It houses your mind. It carries your awareness. It is your first and last home.

8: THE FUTURE OF MONASTICISM

Monasticism has always been a living tradition—one that evolves with the times. From the wandering ascetics of ancient India to the great monasteries of medieval Europe, monastic life has taken on different forms in response to cultural shifts, technological changes, and new philosophical insights. While the core impulse remains—renouncing distractions in pursuit of wisdom—the structures that support it have changed dramatically over time.

As we move deeper into the modern age, we must ask: *What will monasticism look like in the future?*

The world is shifting at an unprecedented pace. Technology is reshaping how we think, work, and connect. Traditional religious institutions are declining, while new forms of spirituality are emerging. The global economy is creating instability, while climate change and artificial intelligence are raising existential questions that monastics of the past never had to consider.

In this rapidly changing landscape, the modern monk is not a relic of the past but a pioneer of a new way of being. The future of monasticism will not be a return to the old models but an adaptation to a world that demands something different.

The Challenges of Modern Monasticism

While monastic ideals remain timeless, the world today presents unique obstacles that traditional monks did not face.

One of the most pressing challenges is the *crisis of attention*. The modern world is designed for distraction. Smartphones, social media, and the constant barrage of information fragment the mind, making deep contemplation increasingly difficult. Where past monastics withdrew from the world to avoid distraction, the modern monk must learn to renounce noise while remaining within society. The challenge is not just external—it is internal, requiring a deep discipline of mind.

Another challenge is the *decline of religious institutions*. In many parts of the world, traditional monasteries are struggling to survive. Fewer people are joining monastic orders, and those that remain often face financial difficulties. While spiritual longing persists, many seekers are wary of dogma, hierarchy, and rigid traditions that no longer resonate with contemporary values.

Technology also poses a paradox. It connects people in ways unimaginable to past monastics, offering access to wisdom from every corner of the world. Yet, it also threatens to erode traditional monastic values. With artificial intelligence automating work and virtual reality creating immersive experiences, will traditional monastic practices still hold meaning? Or will they need to evolve into something radically different?

Despite these challenges, monasticism is not disappearing. It is transforming.

The Evolution of Monastic Models

To remain relevant, monasticism must adapt. The rigid structures of the past—where monastic life required complete withdrawal—may no longer be practical. Instead, new forms of monasticism are beginning to emerge, blending ancient wisdom with modern realities.

One possibility is the **urban monastery**—a model where monks live in cities rather than isolated retreats. Instead of withdrawing from society, they create small, intentional communities that support deep practice while remaining engaged with the world. These communities could be structured as co-living spaces, urban ashrams, or even loosely connected networks of practitioners who live separately but maintain shared disciplines.

Another emerging model is **lay monasticism—** where individuals take on monastic-style vows while continuing to live as householders. This path acknowledges that full renunciation is not an option for many, yet still offers a structured way to integrate monastic values into daily life. Those following this path may commit to a life of simplicity, daily meditation, and ethical conduct, creating a modern equivalent of the monastic order without requiring celibacy or isolation.

Perhaps the most radical shift is the rise of the **digital monastery—**a decentralized, global network of seekers who practice together virtually. With online meditation groups, livestreamed teachings, and virtual retreats, monastic practice is no longer limited to a physical location. Some practitioners may even take monastic vows while remaining entirely in the digital space, living disciplined lives while engaging with wisdom communities across the world.

Each of these models reflects the growing need for monastic values in a changing world. While the traditional monastery may fade, the monastic impulse remains strong—it is simply finding new forms.

The Rise of Post-Monastic Spirituality

Another possibility is that monasticism itself will dissolve into something beyond traditional forms. Instead of distinct monastic communities, spiritual wisdom may become fully integrated into everyday life. In this scenario, monastic values—simplicity, contemplation, and renunciation—would no longer be confined to monks but would permeate society as a whole.

If artificial intelligence and automation reduce the need for constant labor, could society itself shift toward a more contemplative way of life? If digital connectivity makes wisdom teachings available to all, could the structured monastic path become unnecessary?

These questions point to a paradox: *As monastic principles spread, will they still be considered monasticism?* If a world emerges where deep spiritual practice is accessible to everyone, does the need for monasteries vanish?

It is possible that the future of monasticism is not in monasteries at all, but in a world where the values of monasticism become the foundation of a new way of living.

The Role of the Modern Monk in a Changing World

Regardless of how monasticism evolves, its essence will remain the same:

- The pursuit of wisdom over ignorance.
- The cultivation of simplicity over excess.
- The practice of presence over distraction.

The modern monk will not be defined by where they live or what they wear but by their ability to embody these values in a chaotic world. Whether living in an urban monastery, as a digital renunciant, or as a contemplative within society, those who feel the monastic calling will continue to walk this path.

The monastery of the future may not have walls. It may exist in a small apartment, in an online community, or even in the quiet discipline of an individual who chooses to live with clarity amid the noise of modern life.

The world may change, but the monastic impulse will never disappear.

Conclusion: The Choice to Walk the Path

This book has not been about predicting the future— it has been about participating in its creation.

Monasticism is not something static. It is something that adapts, survives, and thrives in new forms. The question is no longer whether monasticism will continue to exist, but how those who feel called to it will shape its next evolution.

For those who resonate with this path, the invitation is clear: Monasticism is not just an idea or a historical relic—it is a living, breathing tradition that is waiting to be reimagined.

If you feel drawn to this way of life, then the future of monasticism is in your hands.

9: THE SHADOW SIDE
OF MONASTICISM

Monasticism is often seen as a pure, noble path, free from the corruption and distractions of the world. It represents wisdom, clarity, and deep spiritual commitment. The monk stands as an emblem of discipline, renunciation, and higher knowledge, seemingly untouched by the chaos of ordinary life.

Yet, like all human endeavors, monasticism is not immune to its own shadows. Beneath its serene exterior, monastic life carries risks—hidden dangers that can turn renunciation into repression, wisdom into arrogance, and discipline into rigidity. Throughout history, monastic institutions have been plagued by scandals, power struggles, and dogmatic rigidity. Individual monks, no matter how sincere, have fallen into delusion, mistaking spiritual progress for self-denial, emotional repression, or spiritual elitism.

For the modern monk, awareness of these pitfalls is essential. Renunciation alone does not guarantee wisdom. Discipline without understanding can become its own form of bondage. By acknowledging the shadow side of monasticism, seekers can walk this path with greater clarity, avoiding the traps that have ensnared many before them.

The Trap of Repression: When Renunciation Becomes Self-Denial

At the heart of monasticism lies the practice of renunciation—the deliberate shedding of attachments that bind the mind. But when misunderstood, renunciation can become mere suppression. Instead of releasing attachment, the monk may simply bury desires, emotions, and instincts, mistaking repression for spiritual progress.

History is filled with examples of monks who have taken renunciation to an unhealthy extreme. Christian monastics in the Middle Ages sometimes practiced self-flagellation, believing that physical suffering would purify the soul. Buddhist ascetics engaged in prolonged fasting and sleep deprivation, hoping to transcend the body entirely. Hindu sadhus have been known to endure painful austerities, such as holding an arm aloft for decades or standing on one foot indefinitely.

While these practices may demonstrate extraordinary discipline, they can also reflect a misunderstanding of renunciation. True detachment does not come from punishing the body but from seeing through the illusion of attachment itself. When monks suppress natural emotions —desire, anger, sadness—without understanding them, these emotions do not disappear; they simply manifest in distorted ways. Repressed desire can emerge as addiction or secrecy. Suppressed anger can harden into cynicism.

For the modern monk, the lesson is clear: renunciation should lead to freedom, not denial. The goal is not to reject life but to engage with it without clinging. Suppression may create the illusion of detachment, but real liberation comes only from deep self-understanding.

The Danger of Spiritual Bypassing

Spiritual practice can be used not only to transcend suffering but also to avoid dealing with it. This is known as spiritual bypassing—the tendency to use meditation, philosophy, or renunciation as a way to escape unresolved personal issues.

A monk who has not confronted their own wounds may use spirituality as a shield, avoiding difficult emotions by retreating into silence or intellectual detachment. They may claim that suffering is "just an illusion" while secretly struggling with depression. They may speak of non-attachment but react with defensiveness when challenged.

This pattern is common in all spiritual traditions. A Buddhist monk may insist that everything is impermanent yet struggle with unresolved grief. A Christian monastic may preach divine love while battling deep loneliness. A Hindu renunciate may declare the world to be *maya* (illusion) while suppressing anger toward their past.

For the modern monk, awareness is key. True spiritual practice does not bypass pain—it brings it into the light. Monastic discipline should not be used to escape emotional work but to deepen self-awareness. Meditation is not a way to numb feelings but to see them clearly. Philosophy is not a means of intellectual detachment but a tool for deeper engagement with reality.

The real test of monastic practice is not whether one can remain serene in solitude, but whether that serenity holds up in the face of life's challenges.

The Illusion of Superiority: When Monasticism Feeds the Ego

Ironically, the very path designed to dissolve the ego can sometimes inflate it instead. When monks dedicate themselves to strict discipline, intense study, or deep meditation, they may begin to feel superior to those who do not. The sense of being on a "higher" path can create a subtle but powerful form of arrogance.

This can manifest in various ways. Some monks adopt an attitude of quiet judgment, looking down on those who live in the world, seeing them as "caught in illusion" while viewing themselves as awakened. Others fall into intellectual elitism, using philosophy to prove their own superiority rather than to cultivate genuine wisdom. Even humility itself can become a disguise for spiritual pride—a monk may appear outwardly modest while secretly taking pride in their renunciation.

Throughout history, many spiritual traditions have warned against this trap. In Zen Buddhism, there is a saying: *"If you meet the Buddha on the road, kill him."* This means that any fixed idea of enlightenment— especially the idea that one has *attained* it—must be discarded. The moment a monk believes themselves to be enlightened, they have fallen into illusion.

For the modern monk, humility is not just a virtue but a necessity. True wisdom does not separate but unites. It does not make one feel superior but dissolves the very idea of superiority. A monk who has truly renounced the ego does not need to prove anything to anyone—including themselves.

The Escape Fantasy: Monasticism as Avoidance

Many are drawn to monastic life not out of wisdom, but out of a desire to escape. The pressures of modern existence—work, relationships, responsibilities—can make monasticism seem like an easy way out. Some seek the monastery not for enlightenment, but as a refuge from personal failure, loneliness, or dissatisfaction with life.

But true renunciation is not about running away. A monk who enters monastic life to escape suffering will quickly find that suffering follows them. Isolation does not erase inner turmoil; it magnifies it. No monastery is free from human conflict, no amount of meditation can silence an unresolved mind, and no spiritual vow can replace the work of genuine self-inquiry.

The difference between true renunciation and escapism is intention. True renunciation is a conscious decision to let go of attachment, knowing that freedom comes from within. Escapism, on the other hand, is avoidance—an attempt to run from life rather than face it with clarity.

For the modern monk, this means asking hard questions: *Am I seeking solitude to deepen my practice, or to avoid something? Am I renouncing the world out of wisdom, or out of fear?* If monastic life is being used as an escape, it will eventually fail. But if it is embraced as a path of engagement—with oneself, with truth, with the present moment—it becomes something real.

The Rigidity of Rules: When Discipline Becomes a Prison

Monastic life is built on discipline. But discipline, when misunderstood, can become rigidity.

Some monks become so attached to structure that they lose sight of its purpose. They follow rules not as a means to wisdom, but as an end in themselves. They obsess over ritual, measuring spiritual progress by adherence to form rather than depth of understanding. This kind of rigidity can lead to guilt, shame, and an inability to adapt.

The great monastics of history understood that discipline must serve wisdom, not the other way around. The Buddha himself encouraged monks to follow the Vinaya (monastic code) but also reminded them that rules should never override common sense or compassion. Monastic practice should be a tool for liberation, not a cage of self-imposed restrictions.

For the modern monk, this means remaining flexible. Disciplinc is necessary, but it should be guided by insight, not fear. The true measure of spiritual progress is not how well one follows rules, but how deeply one understands their purpose.

Conclusion: Walking the

Path with Awareness

Monasticism is not a guarantee of wisdom. It is a path, and like all paths, it has obstacles. The modern monk must remain vigilant—not only against external distractions but against the internal traps of the path itself.

Renounce, but do not repress.
Meditate, but do not bypass.
Be disciplined, but not rigid.
Seek solitude, but do not isolate.
Remain humble, but do not fall into false humility.

Monasticism is not about perfection. It is about walking the path with awareness, knowing that every step—whether forward or backward—is part of the journey.

10: THE PATH OF THE MODERN MONK

The world does not need more followers. It needs seekers, contemplatives, and pioneers —those willing to walk a different path.

The modern monk is not defined by robes, monasteries, or religious affiliations. They are defined by their way of being—a life guided by simplicity, wisdom, and deep presence in a world of distraction. They are not set apart from the world, but neither are they fully immersed in its illusions. They live in the city yet remain untouched by its chaos, engage with society while remaining inwardly free, and walk among others while walking entirely alone.

This book has explored what monasticism might look like in the 21st century—not as a relic of the past, but as a living tradition being reborn. The final question is not whether monasticism will survive, but whether those who feel its call will choose to embody it.

The monastery no longer has walls. The vow no longer requires ordination. The path is open, waiting to be walked.

The Core Principles of the Modern Monk

Throughout history, monastic traditions have been shaped by specific vows and disciplines. While modern monasticism may look different, its essence remains unchanged.

Simplicity Over Excess

To live as a modern monk is to embrace a life of clarity and minimalism, not just in possessions but in thoughts, commitments, and priorities. It is about letting go of what does not serve the path—whether material distractions, unnecessary obligations, or mental clutter.

Presence Over Distraction

Attention is the most valuable currency in the modern world. The modern monk trains the mind to resist compulsive distraction, cultivating awareness in every moment—whether eating, walking, speaking, or working. Instead of being consumed by technology, they use it intentionally. Instead of filling silence with noise, they embrace stillness.

Wisdom Over Ignorance

A monk does not seek knowledge for its own sake, but for liberation. Whether through sacred texts, meditation, or direct experience, the modern monk prioritizes deep learning and contemplation. They are not content with shallow beliefs or secondhand wisdom—they seek direct insight.

Discipline Over Comfort

Freedom is not found in indulgence but in structure. The modern monk creates a life of rhythm and consistency—not out of rigidity, but because discipline creates space for depth. Whether through daily meditation, ethical commitments, or personal vows, they cultivate a structured life that supports awakening.

Service Over Self-Centeredness

A monk does not renounce the world out of apathy, but out of love. True wisdom is not hoarded—it is shared. Whether through teaching, writing, or acts of compassion, the modern monk sees their path as part of something larger than themselves. They are not separate from the suffering of others, but engaged in alleviating it in whatever way they can.

These are not rules. They are principles—guiding lights for those who wish to live with depth and meaning.

How to Walk This Path

The call to monasticism manifests in different ways. Not everyone will walk the same path, and not everyone will commit to it in the same way. Below are three distinct yet overlapping approaches to modern monastic life.

The Solitary Monk: The Path of Deep Contemplation

Some are drawn to a life of retreat, dedicating themselves to intense meditation, study, and self-inquiry. They may live in remote locations, limit social interactions, and structure their lives entirely around the search for truth.

This path is suited for those who feel called to extreme simplicity, solitude, and inner realization. It requires great discipline but offers great depth.

The Householder Monk: The Path of Monastic Integration

Not all monks need to leave the world. Some maintain careers, relationships, and families while still living monastic values. They structure their days with discipline, commit to deep practice, and treat everyday life as a spiritual path.

This approach allows for the balance of worldly engagement and inner renunciation. It is for those who feel called to monasticism but also to participation in society.

The Digital Monk: The Path of Global Connection & Teaching

Some monks use technology to spread wisdom, teach, and build online spiritual communities. Instead of a physical monastery, they create digital spaces where seekers can gather. They take vows of discipline and simplicity while engaging globally.

This path is suited for those who feel called to share monastic wisdom in new ways, using modern tools to foster deep practice and connection.

No path is superior to another. The question is not which is "right," but which is yours.

The Invitation: Choosing the Monastic Path

Monasticism is not disappearing. It is evolving. The new monk will not wear the robes of the past, nor will they necessarily take vows in a temple. Instead, they will be defined by their depth of awareness, their commitment to wisdom, and their ability to live with presence in a distracted world.

To those who feel drawn to this path, the invitation is simple:

- *Live simply, and renounce what does not serve you.*
- *Seek wisdom, and do not settle for illusion.*
- *Cultivate presence, and resist distraction.*
- *Create discipline, and shape a life of depth.*

- *Serve others, and let your practice benefit the world.*

These are not abstract ideals. They are living commitments. To walk this path is not to retreat from life but to embrace it fully—with clarity, with purpose, and with an unshakable dedication to truth.

A New Monastic Renaissance

Monasticism is not just an idea—it is a movement waiting to be reborn.

If this book has resonated with you, then you are already part of that movement. Whether you live in solitude or in a city, whether you renounce the world or engage with it, the choice to live with simplicity, wisdom, and presence is yours to make.

The world is in desperate need of clarity. Those who walk this path are not just helping themselves—they are helping to reshape the future of spiritual practice.

For those who feel inspired, the next steps are personal. There is no single way forward, only the commitment to walk the path in your own way.

If you are ready to step into the life of a modern monk, your monastery is wherever you stand.

BEYOND THIS BOOK

An Invitation to Moksha Sangha

If you've made it to this point, something in this book has likely resonated with you. Perhaps you have long felt drawn to the monastic path but were unsure how to integrate it into modern life. Perhaps the idea of a modern monk speaks to something deep inside you—something that has been waiting for acknowledgment. If so, you are not alone.

The monastic impulse is alive and well. Across the world, people are seeking simplicity, clarity, and wisdom in the midst of an increasingly chaotic world. Many feel the call to a more contemplative way of life but struggle to find a structure that fits the realities of today. The old monastic institutions are fading, yet the desire for a meaningful, disciplined path remains. This is where *Moksha Sangha* begins— a modern, evolving community for those who wish to embody monastic values in a way that is flexible, practical, and deeply rooted in authentic practice.

What is Moksha Sangha?

Moksha Sangha is a lay monastic order and practice community designed for those who resonate with monasticism but do not wish to—or cannot—completely withdraw from the world. It is not a traditional monastery, nor is it a casual meditation group. Instead, it is a structured yet adaptable path, allowing for deep spiritual commitment without requiring rigid adherence to old models of renunciation.

Some who engage with the Moksha Sangha will choose the path of householder monks, maintaining careers, relationships, and personal responsibilities while committing to a disciplined way of life. Others may feel called to deeper renunciation, exploring what a modern monastic order could look like in practice. The Sangha welcomes both approaches, seeing them not as opposites, but as complementary expressions of the same impulse.

At its heart, Moksha Sangha is a space where seekers can support one another in discipline, contemplation, and awakening. It provides a refuge for those who wish to cultivate monastic values without needing to separate from the world entirely.

Is This Path for You?

The monastic path is not for everyone. It requires

discipline, focus, and a willingness to challenge conditioned ways of thinking and living. It is not about escaping life, but about seeing it more clearly. If you feel called to a life of deeper simplicity, self-inquiry, and structured practice, Moksha Sangha may be a place where that calling finds expression.

There is no pressure to commit beyond what feels right for you. Some may explore the Sangha for a time and move on, while others may find that this is the spiritual home they have been seeking. Either way, the invitation is open to those who feel drawn to it.

Where to Learn More

Moksha Sangha is still taking shape. Its form will evolve based on those who feel called to participate. If this vision speaks to you, I invite you to explore it further. Ask questions. Observe. See if this path aligns with your journey.

Visit the official website **www.MokshaSangha.org** to get started. There you can learn more about our vision and find links to join the online community. That's where you can connect with others on the path, make new friends, engage in discussion, and learn more about upcoming opportunities to practice together.

For now, this is simply an invitation—one that you may accept now, later, or not at all. The monastic path is not about obligation; it is about recognizing a call that has always been there, deep within you. If you feel it, you are welcome to explore it with us.

The monastery of the future is not a place—it is a movement. And it begins with those who are ready to live it. If that is you, then your next step has already begun.

ABOUT THE AUTHOR

Zach Perlman (Mokshadas)

Zach became a Hindu monk of the Ramakrishna Order in 2005, and was initiated into Tibetan Buddhism by the Dalai Lama in 2009. He then spent many years working for nonprofit interfaith organizations such as Monks Without Borders, the Philosophical Research Society, and the Council for a Parliament of World Religions. Zach is the author of several books, a contributor to multiple podcasts, and a meditation teacher supporting spiritual seekers around the world.